To Pat & Tim

He said he would write a book and he did!

Fred T. Baker

BIRCHES

BIRCHES

POEMS—VERSES—RHYMES

Fred T. Baker

Copyright © 2007 by Fred T. Baker.

| ISBN: | Hardcover | 978-1-4257-8080-7 |
| | Softcover | 978-1-4257-8068-5 |

All rights reserved. No part of this book may be reproduced or transmitted in any form or by any means, electronic or mechanical, including photocopying, recording, or by any information storage and retrieval system, without permission in writing from the copyright owner.

This book was printed in the United States of America.

COVER ART
From an original oil painting by Alice Ruth Baker.

To order additional copies of this book, contact:
Xlibris Corporation
1-888-795-4274
www.Xlibris.com
Orders@Xlibris.com

ACKNOWLEDGEMENTS

The Author gratefully acknowledges the support and assistance of the following individuals: Alice Ruth Baker, Rosemary Baker-Monaghan, Douglas Patrick Baker, Carrie Ann Julian, Daniel Clinton Baker, Daniel Monaghan, Robert Julian, Zackary Thomas Julian, and John S. Fullerton.

This book is dedicated to Alice Ruth Baker.

*Oh precious wife, my dearest one,
you brought blue skies and Summer sun,
as down the path of Time we strolled,
together young, together old.*

Alice R. Baker, pictured at Birch Bay, Washington, 1967.

CONTENTS

Heroes 1
Parents 2
Wife 3
My Sister, Emogene 4
Birch Trees 6
Attic 10
Wooden Church 11
Childhood Home 12
Homemade Bread 13
Pioneer Home 14
Rich Or Poor 15
Depression Time 16
Zackary 18
Movie 19
Zoo 20
Crossword 21
Crocus 22
Birdfeeder 23
Rain 24
Lightning 25
The Dells 26
Rose Garden 27
Rock Garden 28
The Landscapers 29
Flower Garden 30
Paris 31
Brook 32
Cabin 33
Big Foot 34
Unicorn 35
The Bells 36
Crime 37

Golf 38

Sugar Dog 40

Sugar, The Cat 41

Shoelaces 42

"The Captain Of Our Soles" 43

Dedication to Frank James Baker

 Frank: Remembrances Of An Older Brother 46

 Summer Vacation 48

 Marbles 50

 Nineteen 51

 Away Back Then 52

 Arlington 53

 Clayton 54

 A Voice 55

 Going Home 56

 In The Army 57

 Military Christmas 58

 A War Wages—March 2007 59

Irish Lad 60

Native Land 61

William O. Douglas 62

Meredith Baylor 64

Maude 65

Jim Pruitt 66

Lee 67

Nome Prospector 68

Jason 70

Larry 71

Charlene 72

Walter 74

Sid 75

Soup 76

Mars 77

Rye 78

Camped Out 79

Big Bang 80

Universe 80

Pigeon 81

Chimes 82

Alone 83
Cottonwoods 84
Path 85
Farm & City 86
Neighbor 87
Joe 88
Tugboats 89
Angler 90
Mount Rushmore 91
Rafters 92
Swish! 94
Football Star 96
Gopher 97
Coach's Dream 98
"March-O-Graph" 99
Red-Winged Blackbird 100
Lost 101
Earthquake 102
Volcano 103
Democrats 104
Ambitious 105
Muddy Waters 106
Rhythm 107
Gum Tree 108
Leaves & Trees 109
Apples 110
Fruit Work 111
Avocado 112
Elephant Ears 113
October 114
Haunted 115
To America 116
Thanksgiving 118
Mission 120
Impact 121
Evening Late 122
Brush Prairie 123
First Snow 124
Whistle 125

Snow 126
Winter.. 127
Christmas 128
Christmas Morn 129
Christmas Tree 129
Hitchhiking 130
Party 131
New Year's... 132
Nose For Crime.. 133
Old Sage.. 134
Family Tree 135
Camelot... 136
Britons... 138
Child's Tale 139
Computer... 140
In Rhyme... 141
Purple Shadows.. 142
The Greatest American Poem 143
Remember Me... 144

HEROES

Heroes they are.
Heroes they will forever be.
Men and women who fought
and died for our liberty.
Thousands, now totally
forgotten by name.
Many buried in the earth
where they were slain.
Others missing in the waters
of distant seas.
Lost forever from distraught
and grieving families.

How to honor these patriots
from our vast American lands?
Not just with soaring flags
and blaring brass bands,
proclaim it loudly and often
for all Americans to hear:
Heroes they are.
Heroes they will forever be.

PARENTS

I remember Mother. I remember Dad.
Visiting their gravesites, side by side,
leaves me thoughtful, rueful and sad.

They worked all the time,
seldom, if ever, complaining,
as they raised a large family
through the Great Depression,
as if on a special mission.

And they gave love in their way,
but never would they say it,
but you could always feel it.

Speaking of love,
as I stand over their gravesites,
I can say it to them,
again and again.

WIFE

Nursing me after an accident,
my wife works all day and half the night,
handles numerous tasks, does them right.

This includes nursing duties and medical chores,
dispensing of pills and so much more:
she glows with a spark from dawn to dark,
manages yard work, she cooks, she cleans,
does grocery shopping, collects the mail,
pays monthly bills, keeps records too.

So now you know, it's no surprise,
she is surely an angel in disguise.

MY SISTER, EMOGENE

I retain this childhood scene
of my lovely sister, Emogene,
as a very young, active girl,
she would dance and twirl.

She and a young girlfriend
practiced a dance routine
to be performed a few hours later
in a downtown movie theater.
They brought the house down,
as they danced and bounced around.
But alas, that ended their short careers.
They were told to slow down, poor dears.

Another scene jumps forth quickly,
as this lassie and I, a wee lad,
walked the frigid neighborhood streets
to sell Christmas wreaths, made by our Dad.

Extra Christmas money for the holiday,
each successful exchange was hailed.
The plan was excellent, when it worked,
but left us cold and shivering when it failed.

Entering her high school years,
Emogene suddenly had a new name.
She was now officially called Jeannie,
a popular and well-liked young lady.

Just a few thoughts of sister Emogene,
now thought lovely and pretty as well.
She and Bud raised a remarkable family.
She was a golden princess on Earth,
and welcomed richly in heaven as well.

BIRCH TREES

The Rimrock Lake safety guide
hailed and waved us aside
to check our boat's safety equipment.
Seeing a birthday cake in the boat, he asked,
"What's with the decorated cake?"
"A birthday party and camp-out day," I replied.
"Never seen a decorated cake
in the middle of our lake," he said.
"Where do you plan to camp?"

"We're headed for the grove
of birch trees," I said.
It's worth a mention
they caught our attention,
a preferred spot to camp.
We headed in that direction.

We'd been informed these were shallow-water beaches,
where you walk your boat right up on the sand.

"Who will jump in and wade the boat ashore?" I asked.
"I'll do it," my wife said,
as she bailed out over the side into the water,
where she promptly disappeared.

Her enormous straw hat
floated away askance,
as she burst forth sputtering and gasping.
All others were grinning,
as she swam to bring the boat ashore.

Unpacking, we stacked our skis
against the white-barked birch trees,
handy for our first event,
after setting up the tent.
This was a two-hour session,
just our second lesson,
on the tricky water-skis.

Practice swimming was next,
more like a direct attack
against the lake and back.

Tired now, we were ready
for a picnic lunch and birthday party.
Featured at the venue,
from a gourmet BLT sandwich menu,
was a large pan of bacon
sizzling on the camp stove.

"Hand me that pan of bacon," I said.
A daughter did.
The handle was still hot.
Poof, out of her hand it flew,
bacon cooked through,
especially well-done,
now basking in the sand
under a mid-day sun.

We sang birthday songs,
followed by large slices of cake,
and opened a present or two,
the best that we could do.

Time for a short nap or rest,
whatever suits each best.
I, propped up to write
poems quaint and light.
My wife, deep in artist's oils,
one of her favorite toils.
All others were reading history
or a favorite mystery.

While we worked, read or nodded,
a sudden burst of wind rattled the area
and blew our boat off the island
into the water.

The youngest daughter noticed it first,
"Quick!" she shouted,
"The boat's floating away!"

The older daughter jumped up.
"I'll catch it!" she said,
as she splashed away in pursuit.
Halfway across the lake, she caught it,
our only escape vehicle.

Time to head for home.
Caught our dog, Sugar,
who loved to run and roam.
All was now secured to leave,
with a final salute
to the tall and regal birch trees.

ATTIC

Collected countless treasures
and antiques over the years.
Kept piling these prizes inside
without concern or undue fears.
Finally, I said, "Enough!
The house is stuffed."
But a calmer voice said,
in tones most emphatic,
"All will be safe stacked in the attic."

So time and again,
the bargains galore,
treasures to store,
went through the overhead door
leading to the attic.

The mounds of products sit there still,
purchases of our own free will,
but we're getting frantic
to empty and clean out our attic.

The children are grown,
living on their own,
"Let's reel them in," I said,
"for a long working day
to remove the excesses
and clean up the messes."

It would be a Godsend
if once more we could bend
and freely stand in our attic.

WOODEN CHURCH

They call to us, loud and clear,
that old brown church
and covered bridge of wood,
calling us back
to scenes of our childhood,
to revisit the grassy hills
and the vale of wildflowers and rills.

A return after thirty years,
and the first feature seen
was that the vale was no longer green.
Overcrowding has depressed the entire scene.

Office buildings, highways, gigantic stores,
bridges, byways, new homes galore,
huge parking lots,
and gambling spots;
the small friendly stores
didn't exist as before.

And the disappointing sight
of a concrete structure
that replaced the beloved,
brown, wooden church was a fright.
Also missing was the covered bridge
from the old church road.

We just could not imagine
singing the beloved hymns
we sang so long ago.

CHILDHOOD HOME

Their childhood home structure,
a one-story, older bungalow,
stood in all of it's dismal glory
at the end of a long, similar row.

Repairs by the over-worked dad,
amateur workmanship at it's best,
a crowded place for all to sleep,
to cook, to clean, and all the rest.

Torrid hot in the Summer,
frigid and drafty in the Winter;
always household chores to do
and firewood to cut and splinter.

The house would not win a prize
for appearance, style or show,
but only the close family-members
were in place to actually know
that within the paper-thin walls
was peace, love and true care,
showered on just everyone
privileged to stay and live there.

HOMEMADE BREAD

Just a young boy, I split the wood,
piled it high in a box that stood
alongside of our old kitchen stove.

Every Tuesday, I inserted kindling
into the stove's fire-pit,
struck a match, and the fire was lit.

The oven slowly heated,
as more wood was added.
Nothing was said.
This was the day, each week,
when Mother kneaded the dough,
making it ready for baking
her loaves of homemade bread.

Neighbors knew it, timed visits,
as bread came out of the oven,
steaming hot, heavenly smelling,
ready to slice, big, thick slices.
Mother spread them
with melting butter
and homemade jam.

It always caused appreciative sighs,
made voices utter, "Oh my, that's good!"

It's years later now.
A different home.
We chose the convenience
of store-bought bread.
It's not the same.
No loaves compare.
Never as good as
Mother's homemade bread.

13

PIONEER HOME

He remembers home
in a sparsely settled land,
no frills or fuss,
it simply was grand.

Remembers the hills
that rimmed the place,
rugged, not like now,
showing a gentler face.

Streams flowed swift,
flowers grew wild,
he roamed there adrift,
like a wayward child.

Now, he's back home,
just for a short while;
seeing vast changes
forces a sad smile.

He holds back the tears,
feels the weight of years.

RICH OR POOR

In our isolated Western town during the Great Depression,
if you lived in certain areas you were considered poor.

Not so our gang of boys.

We were cowboys riding night watch on the trail.
Texas Rangers patrolling a long, dusty border.
Canadian Mounted Police chasing fugitives through snow.
Patriots charging with the Green Mountain Boys.
Camped with General Washington at Valley Forge.
Federal agents swooping down on John Dillinger.
With Captain Bly during the mutiny on the Bounty.
Flying with Lindberg through fog and rain over the Atlantic.
Bouncing and rolling in a barrel at Niagara Falls.

We were all this and more,
never considered ourselves poor.

DEPRESSION TIME

Just a young lad in 1935,
he was abundantly alive
with the spirit of Christmas.

It would be a skimpy gift-giving year,
that was crystal clear.
It was the time
of the Great Depression.
The family was poor.
No money available
to do anything more.

On Christmas Morning, he could expect to find:
hard candy, chocolate-covered cherries,
oranges, apples, assorted berries,
plus a variety of nuts,
and one gift under the Christmas Tree.
One gift for each of the family-members
was as far as the money would reach.

After early Mass,
the family enjoyed a light breakfast;
after which, they all gathered
around a small Christmas Tree
mounted on a wooden apple box
for stability and height.
The box was draped
with a red and bright linen cloth.

The Christmas Tree was decorated
with two strings of colored lights,
old-time favorite ornaments,
dangling silver icicle strands,
and colored ribbons tied in shapely bands.

Gifts were distributed, one after another,
with everyone joining the recipient
in the opening ceremony to lengthen the fun.

Now, only the young lad
was left without a present.

The dad said, "Excuse me, be right back,"
and left the room.
He quickly returned carrying a sled,
not brand new, but newly painted red.
"It's for you," he said to the surprised boy,
whose face lit up with joy.

Forever after, the young lad
remembered that Christmas
as the best he ever had.

ZACKARY

Zackary is his name.
Chess is his game.
He will play
anyone,
anytime,
anyplace,
on the computer,
or face to face.

MOVIE

Grandpa and Zack were idling around
near the old movie theaters downtown.
Gramps said it would be groovy
if they had time to see a movie.

But Zack popped out with a question.
"What's the best movie you've ever seen?"
he asked Gramps.

"That's a keen thing to ask,
because I remember clearly,
an excellent movie I loved dearly:
'The Call of the Wild' it was named.
For an adventure tale, it was famed."

"You're too young to know about it,"
Zack was told. "But guess what?
That show is playing down the street.
For an afternoon show, it can't be beat."

"Let's go see it!" Zack agreed.

"Wasn't that the best show you've ever seen?"
Gramps asked Zack.
"No," Zack said.
"My favorite movie is 'Harry Potter'."

ZOO

She was born in a cage on a wintry day,
the last animal to be introduced to the world
at that scraggy old address:
The City Zoo.

It took years of hard work, special drives,
to bring the controversy to the attention of influential persons:
The Zoo was not a fit place for man or beast.

Neighborhood children pleaded to keep it open.
They loved the animals.
It allowed them a touch of the wild,
if only in their imagination.

The children did not have the influence to succeed.
So there it stands, all metal and concrete,
weeds growing over everything,
a sorry spectacle,
and a ridiculous failure of cooperation.

Where is she?
That last animal born in that Zoo?

Nobody knows.

CROSSWORD

It's a simple crossword puzzle,
printed in the newspaper, they say.

Then to work it and finish it,
why does it take me all day?

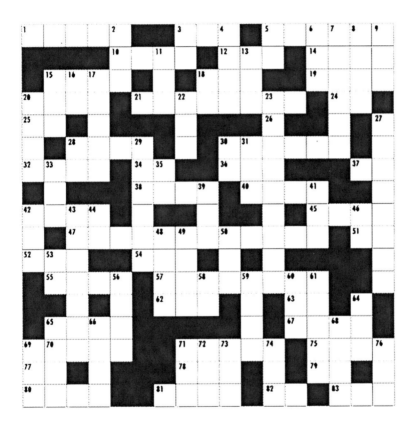

CROCUS

It's still January,
but old friends have now arrived
to chase the gloom.
Favorite flowers, in full color,
not one, but three,
as bright as they can be.
These blooms are not bogus,
they're widely known as crocus.

BIRDFEEDER

It's magical.
Secured to the outside
of our bay window,
a small birdfeeder
of clear, tough plastic,
for a close-up view
of the birds feeding.
What could be neater?
Piled high with bird feeds
and favorite sunflower seeds.

The birds flit, flurry, fuss and scold,
to obtain a fair share,
during all types of weather,
while we watch from inside
in favorite easy-chairs of leather.

Sparrows, house finches,
and small chickadees,
plus a host of rarer breeds,
all searching for a feast,
while inside, warm and rosy,
we're nice and cozy,
enjoying the busy bird scene.

It seems an unfair exchange,
that's what I have to say,
for we replenish their feeder once a week,
while the birds entertain us every day.

RAIN

One individual occurrence
that drives me wildly insane
is the drip, drip, drip of a mild rain.
A violent storm, rain slashing down,
doesn't trigger any undue strain,
like the drip, drip, drip of a mild rain.

When rainwater is gushing,
and violently rushing,
into a street's storm-drain,
I feel no pain. I'm totally sane.
But the drip, drip, drip of a mild rain
just drives me wildly insane.

It's raining now,
can't you hear it drip, drip, drip?

My endurance has peaked.
I'm starting to creak.
Quick! Hand me down my walking cane
to step out into that mild rain.

Soon, I'll be running, jumping, and dancing.
a man possessed.
Searching, ever searching,
for a break in the clouds
and the absence of that mild rain,
that drives me crazy and wildly insane.

LIGHTNING

I've seen a thousand lightning flashes,
heard the loud and thunderous crashes.

But I never heard the violent strike
that smashed me while I rode my bike.

Here's the message I must confide,
the bike and I were electrified.

THE DELLS

In the month of April,
they journeyed to view
a host of blooming flowers
growing wild in The Dells.

Light-hearted, happy,
they enjoyed melodious
ringing of church bells.

Now, flowers or bells
can't erase the dreadful gloom
caused by recent knowledge
of impending cancer doom.

Diagnosed by physicians,
cancer of bodily cells,
she senses the evil lurking,
the deadly ending it foretells.

Once again at The Dells,
they found dead, decaying flowers,
and heard only dreadful,
mournful ringing of the bells.

ROSE GARDEN

She walks through her rose garden alone,
one last time, before moving to an elderly care home.

She steps on decorative stones,
embedded years ago
in the paths of the garden.
She recalls the hard work
and long hours devoted
to establishing her garden,
when she and the garden were young.

Roses became her renowned specialty,
magnificent, prize-winning blooms.
Her show entrants
with blue ribbons were routinely hung;
her cash registers were constantly rung,
when she and her garden were young.

Now, her own natural beauty has faded
in time, as it does on all rose blooms.
Depleted energy and ill-health dictates
a move to a specialty home,
which in the morning now looms.
We will remember her and the good times sung,
when she and her garden were young.

ROCK GARDEN

"Let's go!" he shouts to the family,
"The water level in the river is at a ten-year low.
It's time to gather large river rocks for a new rock garden."

They pick out the shapely, colored stones,
deliver them to the garden site,
arrange them artistically for best effect.
Arrange them again.
Stand back.
Inspect the results again.
Nothing is working.
Four score of rocks cannot lay about.
The best idea is to take them back
where we found 'em.

THE LANDSCAPERS

They installed a classic fountain in our backyard
to instill a bounty of splendor
and a wealth of high regard
and praise for their work;
that's the three landscaper gardeners.

Winding down a long pathway,
they passed under a large, vine-covered arbor
and stepped off onto a red-brick patio
furnished with Adirondack chairs painted a bright red.

The three were returning to this backyard
to restore the water-flow to the fountain for the season.
They accomplished their task, then climbed the steps
to a redwood deck to oversee the total effect.

From that vantage point, they could judge
which of the many trees needed attention,
and how the fertilizer needed to be applied
to maintain a green and healthy grass.

The vegetation in the yard had been pruned,
trimmed on a previous visit.
There wasn't much else to do.

They proceeded up another set of stairs to a balcony,
where they decided on refreshments.
Sipping cold drinks, they agreed this mission was completed.
A great day.

We thanked the three landscapers:
our two daughters and their mother.

29

FLOWER GARDEN

A new flower garden
planned from A to Z,
Astor to Zinnia.
Nothing left to chance.
Conceived like a dance.
Each step measured.
Each step treasured.
Exact color chart.
A place for each
flower to start.
No mix-ups allowed.
Areas precisely plowed.
Choice varieties planted
fresh from the nursery.
Weeds previously removed.
Space clean as a whistle.
Not a weed or thistle.
Planting all done.
Watering with care
under a setting sun.
Had monitored the moon,
not to plant too soon.
Sit back for days,
study the various ways
plants proceed to grow.
All the hard work done,
we enjoyed the garden
under a Summer sun.

PARIS

The last time I saw Paris,
while walking on the banks
of the river Seine,
in a thick fog and misty rain,
I slipped and fell.
Should have been using
my new walking cane.

It's a friend,
my walking cane,
but it's not plain.
Twisted, snarled,
knotted, gnarled,
it's one-of-a-kind,
a miraculous find,
worth it's weight
in solid gold,
a marvel to behold.

I'm recovered now from my fall
with the aid of that walking cane.
It stands in the closet against the wall,
ready to serve the next time I fall.

BROOK

He listened to the babble of the brook
as he wandered through the town;
seemed the babble was telling him
this is the place to settle down.

A picturesque Canadian village
set along the St. Lawrence waterway;
his family left it years ago
for jobs out West and better pay.

Retired, his family deceased, alone,
he was desperately seeking to find
a location with family ancestral ties
to which his spirit could finally bind.

The local library contained old records,
proving his family had once lived in the area.
With this desired knowledge, he went searching for a house
to set up his computer and telephone for working.

At the edge of town he found a cabin
in an attractive green and forested site,
where he can rest, muse and write
children's poems, odes and stories.

He still hears the babble of the brook,
now streaming past his cabin door;
it seems forever to be telling him
he need not wander anymore.

CABIN

The cabin sits on the bank
of the Sol Duc River,
framed by sapling trees
that sway in the breeze,
and decked out in bright colors
from a host of new flowers.

Tired when we arrived,
grumpy, fit to be tied,
but in a few short minutes
we felt like old-time tenants.
Wandering to the backyard,
as bright as a picture card,
we settled into lawn-chairs.

An hour slips quietly by;
we watch a duck family
gliding on the river's cold water.

Everyone is wearing a wide smile,
have for quite a while,
anticipating a picnic lunch,
a welcome treat for the entire bunch.

After dessert, it's back to the lawn-chairs
for a pleasant nap in the sun,
until the afternoon is done.

Purple shadows creep
over the lush, green grass,
which prompts us to move inside
to a warm and bright fireside.

BIG FOOT

Sasquatch is alive,
roaming the high peaks
of the rugged Cascade Mountains,
says the wily hunter Billy Meeks.

He bases his claim on traces found
while scouting around:
huge footprints in muddy ground,
hairy stubble on bushes found.
The best clue yet, a fragrance so foul
it made Billy exclaim, "My word!"

Sasquatch is his name.
Big Feet his fame.
Senses sharp, keen,
smelled, but unseen.

Does Big Foot exist
wandering in the mists
of peak and valley,
lonely, loathsome
and terribly smelly?

Hunt him, if you will,
knowing he is a wild, savage beast
searching for a tasty feast.

UNICORN

I've never had the privilege of viewing a Unicorn.
They exist, this I know; the dictionary tells me so.
"A fabled creature, represented as a horse
with a single, spiraled horn on it's forehead."

I've witnessed a host of Aardvarks, milling around,
a large group of Orangutans, acting unsound;
but never a Unicorn have I seen on land or on the sea.
Can there be something wrong with me?

THE BELLS

For whom should the bells toll?
I did not mow the grass this week.
I did not change the oil in the Chevy.
I did not pay the water bill yet.
I did not buy a certain birthday card.
I did not split wood for the fireplace.
Since I didn't do all these things,
the bells should toll for me.

CRIME

Black is the night, more's the pity.
A dense fog has silently moved in
and settled over the city.

Criminals will work this night,
a prime time for crime, a time for plunder.
Many a business will be split asunder.
Who can stop it? This I wonder.

GOLF

Tee up. Limber up.
Stretch. Stretch again.
"Golf," I tell Jake,
"is a piece of cake."

I'm first up. A practice swing.
Once again.
A player calls out, rudely, I think,
"Hit the ball for God's sake."

Finally, a true swing. Smack.
"Down the middle," I cry.
"In the rough," says pal Jake.

"It's not so tough
to hit from the rough,"
I state boastfully.
Imitating a pro-golfer's style,
I swing smoothly through the ball.
"You'll be needing a sand rake,"
says my good pal Jake.

I've read the advice for this situation,
I quote: "Hit behind the ball
using a lofted wedge; follow through."
Abide by this simple rule
and a nice shot will result.

Rules are made by man,
can be easily broken.
The sand flies askew, but the ball
"rests on the grass by the rake,"
says a smiling pal Jake.

I replace that ball
with a brand new power ball for distance.
I paid plenty for it.
I give it a hit,
watch it as it soars high and then drops.
"Into the course lake,"
states my former pal Jake.

"I'm going in now,
yes, to the clubhouse," I state.
"I'm going in now
with a brutal headache."

SUGAR DOG

Our little white dog,
raised from a pup,
is missing again.
Family-members are
worried that Sugar,
as the pup was named,
cannot be found.
Called the pound.
Not there.

Every so often,
he goes on a spree,
escapes from the yard,
makes his way free—
wherever he goes,
whatever he does,
remains a mystery.

Then suddenly Sugar's back
and he's truly welcomed,
but no hugs are forthcoming
for two things are certain:
He's dead-tired
and sorely in need of a bath.

SUGAR, THE CAT

Our beloved housecat
roams the house at all hours.
Sugar, as the cat was named
by us when we found her,
just a tiny kitten,
all white and lovable.

She roams mostly at night,
when the people are fast asleep,
when all is quiet.

She seizes this opportunity
for acrobatic leaping onto our bed.
The next thing I know,
the cat is perched on my head.

Scat, you white cat!

SHOELACES

My shoelaces are untied.

Should I bend over
and re-tie 'em?

Or ignore the
smirking faces,
as I walk by,
trailing laces?

"THE CAPTAIN OF OUR SOLES"

Another adventure came through the door
of our neighborhood family drugstore:
a contest to collect old leather and shoes
for the military's widespread re-use.

It was a program for schoolchildren.
It was our chance to participate
in the World War II effort.

Groups formed, each with a leader.
Emogene, an eighth-grader, was dubbed
"The Captain of our Soles".

A train of wagons, rolling down the streets,
filling up with boots, shoes and more;
that was her plan.

"Have you any old shoes?" I asked the lady.
"None to fit you," she replied.

The wagons filled as our procession moved forward.
We were in first place after three weeks.
A second place finish seemed so bleak,
but our small wagons couldn't compete
against trucks, driven by parents,
that scoured the rich areas of town
in the final week to win.

In grateful memory of

Frank James Baker

WHO DIED IN THE SERVICE OF HIS COUNTRY AT

Sea, South Pacific Area, U.S.S. Neosho, 8 May 1943 (Presumed)

HE STANDS IN THE UNBROKEN LINE OF PATRIOTS WHO HAVE DARED TO DIE

THAT FREEDOM MIGHT LIVE, AND GROW, AND INCREASE ITS BLESSINGS.

FREEDOM LIVES, AND THROUGH IT, HE LIVES—

IN A WAY THAT HUMBLES THE UNDERTAKINGS OF MOST MEN

Franklin D Roosevelt

PRESIDENT OF THE UNITED STATES OF AMERICA

The following twelve poems are dedicated to
Frank James Baker.

After a childhood of diversified adventures, Frank
joined the United States Navy. He served on the
U.S.S. Neosho in World War II.

He was lost at sea during the historic Battle of the Coral
Sea in May 1942 and presumed dead on May 8, 1943.

His name appears on memorials in Seattle and Yakima,
Washington; at the historic World War II Memorial in
Washington D.C.; and at the World War II Memorial
in Manila, The Philippines.

FRANK:

REMEMBRANCES OF AN OLDER BROTHER

It seemed like older brother Frank
had a new adventure every day.

I remember turtle-racing.
He caught his turtles from the mill ditch flowing nearby.
He chalked a number on each top shell,
dug a line in the dirt surface to form a large circle,
and placed the turtles in the middle.
Pick a number. Place a small bet.
The first to cross over was the winner.

Sent away for an expensive buck rabbit
for breeding purposes. Hired the buck out.
Also raised young bunnies for sale.

Built a wooden airplane with cockpit for one.
Moved the small structure to the slanted roof of a shed.
Climbed into the cockpit.
The plane rolled on roller-skate wheels.
A buddy started him down the slope, over the edge.
Straight down. Crashed. Not hurt a bit.

Constructed huge airplane-style wings
of sliced bamboo sticks and strong, thin paper.
Waited for a windy day,
then ran down a nearby hill, as fast as able,
with wings strapped onto his outstretched arms.
Left the ground for a few moments,
then tumbled into a small crash.

Piled lightweight branches, large tumbleweeds,
and other stuff at the bottom of the slanted-roof shed,
then jumped, as if parachuting into the weeds,
time and time again.

At the request of younger boys,
he built them a rubber-band gun
that squeezed off the bands like a machine gun
using clothespins as triggers. It worked.

Inside the shed, he built his own radio shack;
had earphones and equipment to contact friends.
Learned the Morse Code and radio production.

Captured pigeons. Built pens.
Trained them as homing birds.
Used them for sending messages.

Dug out a huge, deep hole in the garden area,
covered it with an earthen roof;
raised mushrooms in the cool, dark interior.

Finally, at the age of sixteen,
he bought a huge Studebaker sedan
for traveling to work at the local Del Monte cannery.

After graduating from high school
and working to save money,
he left for Arizona to attend a radio school.

In Phoenix, he became interested in
the Lost Dutchman's Mine.
Made several hikes in the area.
Nothing. Ran out of money.

Joined the United States Navy.
Served on a tanker,
lost during The Battle of the Coral Sea.

He is well-remembered. A young life lost.
What a waste!

SUMMER VACATION

In the distant past, school was shut down
for a full three months for Summer Vacation.
A bunch of barefoot boys in tattered clothes ran free.
Watched cowboy and gangster movies for a dime.
Swam in the city pools each morning during free-hour time.
Cooled off hot afternoons in irrigation ditches
that flowed, uncovered, through the city and valley.
Snitched pieces of ice from the ice-delivery truck
when the driver was away.
Mowed lawns and moved irrigation hoses.
Worked in close-in orchards for ten cents an hour.
Kept watch over siblings and the home property
when both parents worked.
Played marble games at all hours of the day.
Played "kick the can" and other games in the evening times.
Gathered for softball games in the vacant lots.
Shot cap pistols and exploded firecrackers
around the 4th of July.
Sneaked into the baseball park
for professional games at night.
Slept over in backyards for ghost stories
and camp-like experiences.

There was more.

These vacation Summers, so busy,
the boys had no time for fears.

But war was exploding around the world,
and these boys would grow into it.
Nothing remained the same.

One-by-one, they aged and entered military service.
After military training, they were sent to join the fight.
Thousands were wounded; many thousands died,
young men who pursued the war for you and for me.
Surely, we must honor this generation of heroes
who won World War II.

MARBLES

It's my seventy-sixth year.
I reminisce,
and remember Jimmy Scott,
the marbles champion
of our primary school.

One hole, nine holes, bullring,
pots, or a simple game of lag,
our marbles ended up in Jimmy's bag.

He won the city-wide tournament
for the primary schools.
His photo, with trophy,
was printed in the town's newspaper.

Many years later,
a photo of Captain James Scott
was printed in the town's paper,
with the sad announcement
that he was "killed in action"
while serving as an Air Force pilot
in the war in Europe.

I had played marbles
with Jimmy many times.
Sometimes he let me win,
a fine boyhood gesture.

Maybe that's why
I remember him.

NINETEEN

He was nineteen,
just nineteen,
not a day more,
the hour he died
on Normandy's shore.

Storming the beach,
cutting a path
through barbed wire,
he fell victim to
murderous crossfire.

He came home,
no more to roam,
a young marine,
still a teen,
just nineteen.

Find him now
under a white cross,
near the scenes
of his childhood.
Check today's date;
he would be seventy-eight.

AWAY BACK THEN

Away back then,
sun-burnt boys in tattered clothes;
movie cowboys, our heroes;
movie bandits and Indians, our foes.
All make believe.

Away back then,
vacant fields and alleys for running,
for baseball and other games.
Hot, treeless lots for sunning.
Not make believe.

Away back then,
timeless time, that lasted forever;
a month seemed a year.
Plenty of time for every endeavor.
You can believe.

Away back then,
it ended abruptly when the War came.
Say goodbye to Alice,
goodbye to Jane.
Hard to believe.

Away back then,
some returned; a few remained
over there and elsewhere.
Another few came home, hurt and maimed.
What's to believe?

ARLINGTON

In Arlington's green acres,
our great heroes lie.

Soldiers, sailors, marines,
and men taught to fly.

They answered the call
and marched off to die.

Row upon row of crosses
mark where they lie.

Simple white crosses
that reach for the sky.

Now, as we look and wonder,
we can only ask, "Why?"

Our young men and women
were sent off to die.

CLAYTON

On shore, Clayton would shout for attention.
A ship-worn sailor, he was prone
to speaking vitriol and hate in any port,
if even a small crowd was gathered.

He sought a better world for mankind.
He would raise a raspy voice
to rant, to rave and to scold.

Anchored at Pearl Harbor,
Clayton fell sick,
passed out on deck.

He was awaiting medical aid,
when he awoke to the noise
of the planes boring in on their first attack.
Clayton struggled to rise up off his back.

He refused medical aid
as he wobbled to his battle station
to help repulse the sneak bombing raid.

He swore, he ranted,
he raved, he scolded,
until the first time in years,
he was lost for more words.

It mattered little,
for on this December date,
Clayton met his final fate.

A VOICE

In a San Antonio tavern,
a man stood up, shouted,
"STOP THE WAR!"

We patrons guzzling beer
pretended not to hear,
so he shouted again,
"STOP THE WAR!"

Finally, he quietly said,
"Thousands already dead,
many, many more ahead."
He shouted once again,
"STOP THE WAR!"

Pointing North toward
Dallas and Fort Worth,
"I'll spread the word,
shout until I'm heard,
STOP THE WAR!"

He left us then that day
to journey on his way.
We lastly heard him shout,
"STOP THE WAR!"

GOING HOME

"Will we be going home soon?"
Military men and women
often ask this question
when posted to an
overseas assignment.

Home.
That magical word,
comforting military personnel
over the ages.
It matters not if home
is a mansion or a hovel.
It's home
when you're all alone
in foreign service.

All memories aside,
home is your pride,
and you would ask
the same question:
"Will we be going home soon?"

IN THE ARMY

In the morning,
in the evening,
he dreams of Home.

In the service,
in the Army,
he pines for Home.

Away from the family
for the first time,
it's a misery for him.
Will he adjust to this
clinging longing?
That's the question
needing an answer
before the Army
sends him back
as unfit for service.

What a shame that would be.
He promptly went to see
the Post Chaplain for help.

Here's what the Chaplain said to him,
"Be a man, son, be a man.
That's the Army's plan for you.
Take just one day at a time
and home-sickness will soon pass.
You'll see."

It did, and he visited places world-wide
instead of going home.

MILITARY CHRISTMAS

Christmas was in the air,
festivities everywhere.
It was Christmas Eve.
Stars sparkled bright,
carolers were singing,
church bells were ringing.

Inside Tom's house,
a tree was trimmed with lights,
ornaments, and silver tinsel.
The family was brimming with glee.

Suddenly, a deafening roar
as shells burst through to the floor.
Tom dove for cover
as bombs exploded all around,
debris covered the ground.

Dreaming was ended.

Tom was in Iraq,
and the heat was oppressive
as his fighting unit repulsed the attack,
drove the insurgents back,
here in the heart of Iraq.

A WAR WAGES—MARCH 2007

Everyday, you hear the grim totals
of civilians and American service personnel
killed in Iraq.

It is the deadliest section
of earth in the World.
Will the mortal battles ever stop?

The American President doesn't know.
The American Congress doesn't know.
The American citizens certainly don't know.
The World's media-people don't know.

So, when you ask me that question,
all I can say is,
"I don't know."

IRISH LAD

He was an orphan boy
living on the Emerald Isle
with a feisty Irish family.

At an early age,
he was sent out to sea
where he learned to fight
the British at every opportunity.

After one engagement,
he was forced to flee
out of Ireland
to the Scottish Highlands.

After a couple of years,
he was accepted
into a Scottish clan,
where he grew to be a man.

He was looking for adventure again.
He found a berth
on an American ship
destined for Virginia.

His timing was perfect.
He joined the forces of
General George Washington
traveling to Yorktown
to entrap the British Army.

After the surrender,
the young Irishman
finally felt Free.

NATIVE LAND

"Breathes there the man, with soul so dead,
Who never to himself hath said,
This is my own, my native land!"

This statement, written centuries ago,
cannot be stated by the majority
of Americans who emigrated
to America by the millions
to populate this grand country.
This is *not* their native land.

They can, however, take heart
in those other immortal words written,
"Give me your tired, your poor,
Your huddled masses, yearning to breathe free."

That's what America offers them today.

WILLIAM O. DOUGLAS

Horace Greeley said,
"Go West, young man."

William O. Douglas said,
"Go East, young man."

And he rode the rails
East to New York City
to further his education.
With scarcely a flaw,
he earned degrees in law
at prestigious universities.

And he always remembered
his early childhood days.
A young boy in the West,
family finances a mess,
due to the early loss
of a supporting father.

Hardships of the poor,
seemingly forevermore,
capped by a serious bout
of dreaded polio.
William conquered this
with physical therapy,
administered at home,
and an insistence on roaming
the lower hills and higher peaks
of the Cascade Mountains
for days at a time.

Combine this with high
scholastic achievement,
debating excellence, and
he was ready to tackle the East.

Up through the ranks,
teaching and practicing law,
what qualified people discerned
was what the President saw,
without any obvious flaw,
that William O. Douglas
was ready and able
to interpret Constitutional law.

Nominated for a seat
on the United States Supreme Court,
he was subsequently approved as a Justice.

After years of service,
William O. Douglas became a writer of books
including the bestseller,
"Go East, Young Man."

MEREDITH BAYLOR

This young woman had big dreams:
to swim faster than anyone before;
to compete against the world's bold;
and return home with Olympic gold.

She worked months with a famous coach,
harder than she had ever worked before.
Night and day, day and night,
the training schedule was never light.

Boarded a plane for the Olympic site,
won her preliminaries, left and right.
On national television, she appeared;
jumped out on top, as the others feared.

Did she win the race? you ask bold.
Did she finish first and win the gold?
The result is printed in the record book.
Look to the book, you are brashly told.

MAUDE

Little Maude, a gal, a pal,
ran everywhere with us boys.
Years later, back in that town,
I asked if Maude was still around.
"She's resting in the county jail," a voice said,
"from the most recent drug bust."

Made a visit to the local jail,
found a woman distraught and frail.
Maude's face was wan and pale,
as I walked in and paid her bail.
She was off drugs, was her sworn tale.
To help her more, I would only fail.

My visit to town was for just a day,
a sale completed, I was on my way.

JIM PRUITT

He studied the land
devastated by eons of geological time,
with a circle of low, rugged mountains
watching over it.

An arid desert, with an underbelly,
flattened and sloped into a wide valley.
A land that was buried under countless lava flows,
gutted by ice sheets, carved by wind-blows.

Jim Pruitt was interested,
because a river ran through it.

Fertile topsoil, he recognized with a glance.
The whole valley a garden, if given a chance.

Water for irrigation was the key
to unlock a gravity flow system,
in his mind he could see.

It would work perfectly,
and he knew it,
because a river ran through it.

A hundred years later,
the valley is the pride
of a farming district
miles and miles wide.

The central city is named Pruitt City,
after the first settler who visualized it all,
because a river ran through it.

LEE

Lee often wondered, thoughtfully,
why he had never gone to sea.
He studied the voyages of Captain Cook complete,
but a sea captain he has yet to meet.

Perhaps his great athletic ability
forced him to face life's reality.
Professional baseball is Lee's game,
brought him riches and national fame.
Yet, late at night, the oceans call.
Would he ever leave baseball?

And what would Captain Cook advise?
And would his decision be so wise?
He never witnessed a baseball game,
heard the applause and loud acclaim.

A sea captain is fortunate, they say,
with full benefits and retirement pay.
But for what baseball is paying Lee,
he cannot afford to go to sea.

NOME PROSPECTOR

The gold prospector of Nome
had deserted his Seattle home.
He remembers the exact date
in eighteen hundred forty-eight.

Why he had vacated in a hurry,
aboard an ocean-going ferry,
has never been revealed,
in fact, has been concealed.

Prospected for years all around,
no rich vein of gold ever found,
so when a gambling bet paid big,
he purchased a horse and rig.
A buggy plush, stylish in fact,
from its front to its high-peaked back.
Close friends seemed impressed,
others were somewhat depressed.

But the gold prospector of Nome
in his plush buggy liked to roam.
He approached a dance-hall queen,
the beautiful Shelly McKean.

Offered her a ride in his new rig,
but to her, he was an insignificant pig.
She said, "No!" then changed her mind,
like women of her special kind.

She forever maneuvered to be seen;
in this she was judged to be keen,
so she decided it could be lucky
to ride in this magnificent buggy.

The two were always together,
the queen and her new chauffer.
So when the miners began to go home,
she stayed with the prospector of Nome.

But the plush rig went out-of-style,
and the horse died after awhile.
Shelly's beauty faded over the years,
bringing her very often to tears.

The prospector, Shelly, and the rig
were treated like an unwanted relic,
members of a now senior age
waiting to get off life's stage.

JASON

Jason Brown, a beekeeper
and honey-gatherer,
was often heard to say,
"I'm as busy as a bee."
He thought it was hilariously funny,
since his work was gathering honey.
Yet, he said it with a frown, never a smile.

As it happened, while attending church one Sunday,
Jason met a Christian lady.
In three months time, he was newly wed,
years of loneliness shed.
Now, Jason is still heard to say,
"I'm as busy as a bee."
He says it with a smile, never a frown.

LARRY

Larry was obsessed with the name Larry.
He loved it, but one was not enough.
He went to court to change his name.
Legally, Larry Larry he became.

He had long wished he would marry,
so there would be a Mrs. Larry.
This did not happen over the long years,
so naturally, he began to seriously worry.

Not a descendant to carry on his name
and only the lack of a wife to blame.
Constant worry, wretched worry, all in vane;
some people believed he was going insane.

Larry was convinced he would die
and the name Larry would share his demise.
In a lucid hour, he wrote his epitaph:
Here lies Larry Larry, never able to marry.

CHARLENE

Charlene, Charlene,
oh, precious Charlene,
an unborn child,
as yet unseen.
In early pregnancy,
her name was selected,
as her birth date
was clearly expected.

But problems arose,
and divorcing parents
shared a notion
to end this new life
with an abortion.
Grandparents said,
"No! It would be obscene
to end the life of this human being."

At the time of birth,
these elders stepped forth,
would raise the baby
for all they were worth;
love and cherish her
through the long years;
guide and protect her
from life's many fears.

Charlene was eager to learn,
quick to read;
at an early age, was able
to excel and to lead.
Natural athletic ability
aided her in this cause,
while coaches, teachers,
elders, led the applause.

All were pleased.
It was said at the start
that Charlene was truly gifted,
was exceptionally smart.
But all were amazed
when Charlene reached for the stars
and became the first Astronaut
landed on Mars.

WALTER

From his hospital bed,
Walter gazed out the window;
he counted four leaves
clinging to a barren tree.

Somehow, he associated
the dangling leaves to his life,
once flush with friends,
family-members and wife.

One-by-one, they had passed
to a mortician's care;
now, his Tree of Life
had few leaves to spare.

Suddenly, a leaf fluttered
and fell from the tree;
Walter turned pale, gasped,
and then there were three.

SID

There lies Sid,
in life demented,
wrapped in gowns,
and cheaply scented.

He's dead of course.
To make matters worse,
nobody has filed claims
for his mortal remains.

A pauper's grave
is all that's left;
for proper attention,
Sid is bereft.

He left home
and family behind,
chose powerful drugs
that blew his mind.

Nothing to do.
Too late to save.
Just place poor Sid
into his grave.

SOUP

John Longly remembered it
as New Year's Day of a long time ago
that he stood in a long line of hungry and shivering people.
When hours later, he reached the head of that line,
he was served a bowl of watery soup and a hunk of white bread.
This was back in 1937, in the years of the Great Depression.

On that day, there was snow on the ground,
no jobs to be found.
Depressed by months of unemployment,
he had come to the City to find work.
There wasn't a job for him;
his future appeared grim.
So he wandered the roads and rails,
back and forth across America,
for whatever that was worth.

His prime working years came and passed.
He wallowed in tramp camps and self-pity,
until once again, he was in New York City.

He remembered that New Year's Day of long ago.
To himself, he muttered, "I can always die."
And he did.

MARS

Send the Rovers to Mars,
let the vehicles roam,
explore the arid surface,
transmit the data home.

Determine if water ever was present;
did it stream and flow?
Could life have once existed?
The scientists are eager to know.

Earth-life bubbled in water
many millions of eons ago.
Did this also occur on Mars?
If so, when did the water leave?

Hubble discovered oxygen
on orbs soaring in space.
There are millions in the Cosmos
for people of science to face.

Should we abandon desolate Mars
and direct resources elsewhere?
Are there projects needing funds
that represent better fiscal welfare?

RYE

There is excitement in store for this Summer night.

A spectacular meteor shower is predicted, that's right.
Thousands of shooting lights, soaring and flashing,
as they burn and unravel,
over the farm's vast and magnificent fields of rye.

The absence of cloud cover,
a matchless clear air view,
means we'll watch the shower
as time passes to a wee hour.

We'll enjoy the warm weather in comfort,
the light show in awe,
as the rare display continues in every direction,
over the farm's vast and magnificent fields of rye.

CAMPED OUT

By firelight, camped out at night,
we studied the heavenly stars,
the planets too, adorning the view,
especially Venus and Mars.

"Who placed them there
with wondrous care?"
asked the Three Wise Men from afar.

The shepherds, too,
puzzled by the view,
accepted them,
but wondered, too.

"Who placed them there
with wondrous care?"
we campers asked
and wondered, too.

BIG BANG

The Universe started
with "The Big Bang,"
scientists say.

"Where was the Universe
before the 'The Big Bang'?"
that's what I say.

UNIVERSE

How could the Universe
be here forever?
No beginning as such—
that's simply not clear.

PIGEON

Harold Pender often pondered
and struggled with the vital question:
Will he be accepted into Heaven,
if he belatedly embraces religion?

Or is it abysmally late,
for him to change the message on his slate?
A glorious afterlife, as promised by religion,
or will he be just another dead pigeon?

CHIMES

The man remembers
in his childhood
strolling down a clean, weed-less path
with his mother and father
to a large wooden church
in the green, grassy woods.

Chimes were softly ringing;
a church choir inside singing.
Souls were being saved.

Years later, he's strolling
down that path again,
spying the towering steeple
peeking through the grassy way.
The path is now crumpled and weedy.
His sinful past dim and seedy.

Will he hear the chimes softly ringing,
the church choir inside singing?
Can his soul be saved?

ALONE

The old man listens,
as rain rushes in
and noisily pours
over the city.

Leaves scatter,
as wind gusts blow;
raindrops splatter
against his window.

He peers out,
through the single pane,
relishes the sound
of pouring rain.

A stormy night,
first of the season;
he delights in it
for a curious reason.

A friend has arrived
to visit at last,
unlike acquaintances
from his past.

A visit now,
and storms will reappear,
as he searches
for solace his final year.

COTTONWOODS

Wandering alone, to the old river,
past memories guiding his steps,
he shakes with a sudden shiver,
recalling the recent loss of his wife.

He visits the site of their first home,
a short walk from the wide river,
more an excuse just to roam,
to relieve a loneliness feeling.

He approaches the old wooden trestle
that spans the width of the fast-flowing stream,
that bridges across to a grove of thistle,
and a host of cottonwood trees.

Stepping out to cross beam-to-beam,
he slowly passes over the river;
recalls how she counted each beam
when she crossed over the stream.

Reaching the shade of the cottonwoods,
she would unpack her picnic bag
and lay out a spread for lunch.
All this, he fondly remembers.

Leaning now against a cottonwood tree,
he notices that the tree is trembly,
weak and wobbly as he.
From his grief, he will soon be free.

PATH

She pauses by the river
flowing swiftly through
our industrial town,
past the empty buildings
with the factories,
now all shut down.

Separation of working families
is the town's most recent history.
Why the mills closed down
is no longer a mystery.

Overseas they had moved,
quickly packaged and sent,
leaving our workforce
anxious for the future,
bitter, meager and bent.

Who's to blame? she asks silently,
as she pauses by the rushing river.
NAFTA and other world-trade plans,
she says with a cold shiver.

FARM & CITY

Jennifer peered down
from the family farm
into the lights of the city.
She dreamed of transferring to a town job
to enjoy the city living.

Matthew peered up
from the mansion house
into the distant countryside.
He dreamed of moving out of the city
to enjoy the country living.

Jennifer's days were filled
with farm duties, grooming horses,
cooking and cleaning for hired hands.
A full-time job.
She was not happy.

Matthew spent long hours
preparing briefs and court documents
in his family's law business.
A full-time job.
He was not happy.

Will they do what's right,
or continue present ways of life?

NEIGHBOR

I tried to know my neighbor,
but he was a private man,
refused to divulge much of his past life.

But I ferreted out enough to learn
that he came to California
after working in the silver mines in Nevada.

In California, he panned for gold
and eventually settled for a job
as a bank security guard in San Francisco.

He retired then to the Mohave Desert
and became a virtual hermit.

That's all I learned about that man,
but he learned even less about me,
his closest neighbor.

I, too, was a hermit.

JOE

We went hiking today,
with our treasured dog, Joe,
on trails and paths,
through woods we knew from long ago.

Joe's not as spry
and frisky as he once was.
His stamina, we used to tout,
is now very much in doubt.

We're slower too, Alice,
as we search for the easiest trails.
The woods thicker,
the paths steeper than remembered,
from when Joe, you, and I were young.

TUGBOATS

The man and wife strolled down to the river
to watch the tugboats gliding by.
Some boats moved up-river through the strong current,
with needed products to re-supply.
They remembered their own tugboat
battling these swift currents
during their young and adventurous years.
Their boat is long gone from the water.
Only in memory does it appear
as they gaze out over the water
with thoughts of those many past years.

Now, strolling along the river's bank,
where once they had hurried and bustled along,
their energy faded by time,
they're singing a slower song.

ANGLER

The water in the river sparkled, gurgled and spewed
as Roger flicked out a fly-line
to drift with the current.

Roger was not a dedicated angler.
His attention strayed to a host of flowers
blooming wild across the stream.
He sighed with deep contentment.

Just then a fish took the floating fly.
The reel began to spin,
as Roger stumbled about,
stayed upright, kept the line tight,
and to his surprise saw the fish rise.
In minutes, the catch was landed.

But Roger was not a dedicated angler.
Once again, he glimpsed the colorful flowers
across the stream.
He sighed again,
released the fish into the cold water,
then casually glanced into the blue sky.

MOUNT RUSHMORE

We motored by car,
across Western states,
from Seattle to South Dakota
to visit Mount Rushmore,
the Presidents' sculptures to view.

Washington, Jefferson, Lincoln and Roosevelt:
four faces sculpted out of rock surfaces
on thrusting towers soaring above all.

Boring, blasting, chipping, sanding,
for a host of years,
to demanding measurements
only the designer had known.

A scenic wonder.
We stand and stare.
No sculptures in the World can compare.

RAFTERS

The boating crowd was out.
A grand morning for a wild ride
down the rugged and dangerous rapids,
made four times more difficult
by the melting snow runoff.

Their plans, however, did not include a boat;
a huge rubber raft was the choice
for the ten-mile descent.
This group of men and women
were amateur rafters,
overmatched by the torrent,
but they didn't know it.
Excited, without a clue as to what faced them,
they made preparations to enter the swollen stream.

Four men. Four women.
They were the earliest group out,
and missed the advice and warnings
the later rafters would have offered.

They shoved off.

It was several bends in the river
before they reached white water.
At first, a gentle splashing against the sides of the raft;
soon, small streams began to tumble over the sides
and water entered the boat.
That's when they hit the first violent rapids.

Crashing and rumbling,
the waves mounted the sides of the raft
and poured into the boat.
They had buckets for bailing, but rapidly fell behind.

Spilling headlong into the frenzied current,
the raft uplifted
and dumped everything and everybody
into the cold, rushing water.

Swim or drown, float and be found.
Fortunately, all had quality float-suits on.

Four miles down the river,
they found a slow-water shelter
where they could climb ashore.

Hours later, they were back upriver to their cars.
They said they would never return.

SWISH!

All coaches around
love that sound,
Swish!

Sweet realization the ball,
traveling high and long,
flies straight through the netting.
Eliminates the fretting
as three points are recorded
without a fight for a rebound.

Our team is sizzling,
headed for the year-end tournament,
Holy Cow! What an achievement.
For the first year in twenty,
we'll experience no year-end bereavement
before the tournament starts.

Practice. Swish!
Dropping through netting
with grateful regularity
and fan popularity.
Our total game points
have risen twenty digits
as we advance to the district playoffs.

First opponent ranked higher
with speed and excess height
to be banked on for an early lead.

But we're sizzling,
our shots are swishing
as we cruise to victory.
Our team sails on to reach
the championship game.

The game starts,
moves quickly to half-time
with a tie score.

During half-time, the coach stresses
the three-point shot set-ups needed
for our best shooter Del Crandell.

All went well for hot-shooting Crandell.
Crown us the champs.

Swish!

FOOTBALL STAR

A football star at a college out West.
Widespread fame, one of the best.
His records to last many long seasons.
Popular on campus for many reasons.

A rich man's daughter sought him as a mate.
Married on campus. It seemed to be fate.

Largely unnoticed, this grid-iron star's
scholastic achievements were not up to par.
He made graduation, barely squeaking by,
joined her dad's firm, his fame to apply.
Customers were leery. He did not fare well.

Wife proclaimed that fame lay in the past.
In matrimony, her devotion did not last.
Divorce became final. He lost his plush job.
Moved like a shadow, shunning the grid-iron mob.

Many years later, football numbers intact,
he was invited to a half-time presentation
where he was introduced to new, young fans.

When his feats and statistics were revealed
he spoke to the crowd.
Introduced his new wife and two bright children,
the interest of his life.
Then this aging grid-iron star
was humbled and proud, shed a tear,
when the fans rose up to cheer.

GOPHER

Jamey Miller was the football team manager,
chosen by the team players.
He tried to be a player,
but failed to make the roster.
But, in the role of manager,
he thought himself a gopher.
Go for this. Go for that.

He was constantly busy,
but he was not happy.
Playing the game was his goal.

Before the season was underway, he quit.
Just walked in and said he was through.

"You'll never be a player on this team!"
the angry coach said.

But he was wrong.

One year later, Jamey signed up for the team again,
sixty pounds heavier, two inches taller, and fast.

"Who's that kid?" the coach asked his assistant.
"That's Jamey Miller," the coach was informed.
"He's our new running and passing quarterback!"
the coach said.

COACH'S DREAM

The coach's lifetime dream:
defeat college's number one football team.
The schedule is set.
Is this the time for the coach to say,
"Victory is mine!"

Pack up. Get ready. Follow the team
to the storied football stadium
for this widely publicized, sold-out game.
A golden opportunity for national acclaim.

Boisterous, ready, our unbeaten team
was smarting from the lack of national esteem.
Despite the skimpy odds that they could win,
the team was convinced,
and believed the coach's spin
that they would win,
and the highest ranking would be theirs
at the end of the fray.

Played their very best. Earned a long rest.
And what's more, a very close score.
But they lost, that's crystal clear.
A result none of us wanted to hear.
But we remained true, optimistic as ever,
as we shouted together,
"Just wait until next year!"

"MARCH-O-GRAPH"

In his weekly Sales Meeting,
the Sales Manager boasts:
"I make up a planning sheet every morning
of all the accounts to call on that day."

"I call it my 'March-O-Graph'.
It keeps me organized.
With it, I feel like I'm in a sales army
marching to Victory.
A sales soldier in an army of sales.
Marching. Marching to win!"

"Every salesman needs
a March-O-Graph every day;
don't you agree?
Now, what do you all say
about a March-O-Graph?"

In unison, the sales staff replies,
"We hate the March-O-Graph
and so do our wives and children."

RED-WINGED BLACKBIRD

There once lived a bonnie boy,
the new parents' pride and joy,
but the infant's heart was wrong;
he could not live for very long.

Yet, he was sensitive and alert,
responding to voices in the room
and to calls, distinctly heard:
the outside, shrill notes
of a red-winged blackbird.

Weeks passed.
The babe's life stretched into the Fall season.
Calls of the blackbird were given as a reason.
Now, frail and failing.
The boy's months totaled but seven.
The calls of the blackbird escorted him to heaven.

The ethereal bird
had nested nearby for all those months.
Now, it's calls were not heard
as time passed into tomorrow.

LOST

A frantic search was on for a little girl named Mary,
lost near Eagle Crest Lake.

Elderly John Stokes volunteered to help in the search,
but preferred not to follow others at their fast pace,
wanting to move slower, traveling by himself.

Weather was turning sour,
colder by the hour,
as he trampled through the tall weeds growing wild,
looking for the child.

Time for a break at the Eagle Crest cafeteria,
where he was told
the trail had grown cold.
No sign of the child.
Family now frantic, wild.

Renewing his search,
he followed the lake's shore.
He was humming a sad tune,
while speaking out more.
"Shoreline, please tell me,"
he muttered, "where can she be
in this jungle of tall trees, weeds,
thick bushes and reeds?"

Suddenly, he heard a wee voice.
It stopped him cold.
He stepped forward, bold,
"Are you there, dear?" he said.

"Yes, I'm here," she said.
Barely able to hear, he added,
"Step this way, Mary."
He coaxed her near,
"I'll take you home now."

EARTHQUAKE

Wall mirrors cracked, from side to side,
as an earthquake struck us, valley-wide.

Huge groundswell cracks tore roadways asunder,
bent railroad tracks with pressure from under.

City water-mains burst, the power system failed,
just as the media announced looters would be jailed.

Gas lines ruptured, and numerous fires spread quickly;
a huge financial loss, damages in the millions most likely.

How could this all happen in our peaceful farming valley?
Damages soaring beyond belief, with loss of lives still to tally.

A dozen lost from the city's crew and the volunteer helpers, too.
To rebuild the town structures, we'll need to start anew.

This disaster proves, once again, we're never completely immune
from the fury of nature—a song with a powerful tune.

VOLCANO

The mountain erupted
with a tremendous roar,
lightning flashes,
thunderous crashes.

An enormous cloud of hot ash
poured out and darkened the sky.

Seventy miles away,
ash floated down
and covered the ground
up to five inches.

Total grey was everywhere.
A major clean-up would cost millions.

Can you imagine the total destruction
if a major peak like Mount Rainier,
near the population centers of Washington state,
would erupt?

DEMOCRATS

The democratic faithful are ready to fight;
a debate scheduled for this very night.
Nine are competing for the right
to represent the party in the upcoming Presidential fight.

Stage is lighted, audience is seated,
candidates are announced and suitably well-feated;
lined up across the stage, just moments left to prepare
for the questions forthcoming.
Be ready. Beware!

Spill out your answers. Don't hesitate.
Sensible answers will determine your fate.

Queries are ended, the audience relaxed;
no candidate excelled, none will be axed.
Six more debates are scheduled, all have agreed;
one candidate needs to stand out to succeed.

Primary elections will help the selection
until one person is left standing:
notably, the Official Democratic Candidate.

AMBITIOUS

The candidate appeared,
on local television screens
when running for office.
We marveled at the look of him.

Impeccably attired, pressed, clean,
he introduced himself by the familiar name, Manfred Green.
He purchased adequate television time,
so he was prominently seen.

A state senator for many years,
his sights were set on the national scene.
Ambitious, well-read, a clear spokesman;
his campaign slogan: a simple "Vote Green!"

The consensus of the voters was that
it was time he ran for a national office.
Impeccably attired, pressed, clean,
he was the pride of his political party.

Interested, big-city media began to screen
the private life of Manfred Green.
In business matters, he was cruel and mean.
In religious morals, he appeared unclean.

When they published this news
and added slanted editorial views,
Manfred's stock took a dive.
He lost heart to strive.
And, with energy lost,
from the race he signed off.

Now, when Manfred Green
on the streets of our town is seen,
we scoff and marvel
at the unkempt look of him.

MUDDY WATERS

Jerry says his thoughts are crystal clear;
he has nothing to fear.
The group will discuss and debate subjects like
economics, religion, travel,
outer space, politics, geography,
a current best-selling mystery,
or an event from history.

Free discussion begins.
As usual, Jerry jumps right in.
He charges boldly
to the very heart of the matter,
sharp, keen, pertinent,
with clever and knowledgeable patter.
Just as he reaches a brilliant peak,
shining as he speaks,
suddenly, as in recent weeks,
a mental blackout engulfs him.

His ship of knowledge
has struck an enormous iceberg
and quickly sinks into what Jerry refers to as
those "awful, scary, muddy waters."

It's murky. It's dark.
He stutters. He stammers,
as if pounded by hammers.

His share in the discussion ends.
His brain is stalled,
turned to a stony silence;
once again a victim of
those "awful, scary, muddy waters."

RHYTHM

Jody White has wished, for countless years,
that he would suddenly possess rhythm;
that he would glide across a room
with obvious and admirable grace and rhythm.
No jerks, no sags, or unseemly wobbles.
Just a magical slide, so cool, so smooth,
so sublime it would open people's eyes.
Then, at dancing he would shine,
be compared to a rare wine,
and create for all a magical time.

In truth, he possessed no action
approaching graceful movement.
His feet were heavy, gripping tightly to every floor.
His dance partners never asked for more;
some even leaving, when Jody appeared at the door.
He usually heaves a big sigh,
and wonders why dancers pass him by.

GUM TREE

Towering, regal and stately,
a tree to be remembered.

But the gardener hates the tree;
it's despicable to him, you see.
He doesn't recall its official name,
but it's a gum tree, just the same.

When leaves in Autumn fall,
this tree does not heed the call.
It maintains a firm hold
on dangling leaves, ugly, old.

Through October, November,
December, January, February,
the leaves cling by the thousands,
interrupting the gardener's chores.

In the Spring, when the gardener
is ready and geared up to start
planting new gardens from his cart,
these leaves commence dropping,
show no preference for stopping.

Now they fall, grossly withered,
dappled brown, soggy, moldy.
Raking his new garden patches,
bagging the leaves up boldly,
the gardener sighs, "It's a big job,
really deserves a clean-up mob."
He breathes deeply, wants to shout,
"I should be putting new plants out!"

The tree is a Springtime nuisance,
bothersome, as you can plainly see.

LEAVES & TREES

Fall storms gather,
blustery winds scatter
the leaves
from a host of trees
growing on his property.

That's when he monitors
the variety of yard trees:
smoke tree, hazelnut, birch, gum,
walnut, dogwood, apple, plum,
olive, mountain ash, pine, cherry,
sumac, spruce, and a host of arborvitae.

It takes weeks to rake
and bag the leaves,
to set the bags out front
for the city pick-up crew.
That's when he starts the pruning.

APPLES

An army at attention,
the apple trees stand.
Row after row,
now blossoming
and scenting the land.

In the fertile Yakima Valley,
many apples are grown.
Generations of families
in the process are sown.

Some say bring forth hardcore industries,
with higher-paying jobs and a different history.

Let them stroll down the floral lanes
on a warm day in Spring,
when blossoming buds
prompt the birds to sing.

FRUIT WORK

The mid-afternoon sun
beat down on the workers,
as they finished up their day's work
in the orchards of the Yakima Valley.

It was important for them
to find a little time for a swim
in the Yakima River
that flowed through the Valley.
This brief, refreshing dip
was the only chance to bathe
and clean up for the evening.

Paid minimum wage
for this strenuous work,
most of the family
was forced to join in by the grower.
Young boys and girls
were earning money for the first time.
It gave them an opportunity
to buy clothes, shoes, records and players.

This was 1940.
We had not yet suffered Pearl Harbor.
But the war came.
Orchard workers were hard to find.

Contracts with migrant workers
would never be the same.
Housing
would never be the same.
Migrants were living in unsanitary conditions.
Tents at best.
Now they were leaving
to work in the industrial factories.

Agriculture in the Valley
would never be the same.

AVOCADO

There is one color
I hold in contempt.

At the paint store
they identified it as
Avocado.

Just an amateur painter,
I made the mistake
of choosing that color,
Avocado,
to paint a house
I purchased in Colorado.

Not a true green,
a true shade of green
is never seen,
when you choose
Avocado.

What is it?
I cannot tell,
but from my
ladder I fell.

Blame it all on
contemptible
Avocado.

ELEPHANT EARS

Every year,
he goes with his family
to The State Fair.

Every year,
he sing-songs the following words:
"Elephant Ears!
Elephant Ears!
All I want
are Elephant Ears!"

OCTOBER

October is here,
that glorious time of the year.
You can't escape it anywhere.
You sense it,
experience it,
here, there and everywhere.

Brilliant, shining trees,
imbued with red, brown,
and golden leaves
that are dropping and swirling
in the pleasant breeze.

Harvested crops
adorning the produce shops:
apples, pears, pumpkin, squash,
tomatoes, cucumber, grapes,
last of the corn,
and melons galore,
nuts on the ground,
easily found,
dry, yellow weeds
dropping their seeds.

Irrigation water is off,
lawn implements stored;
plenty of work,
no time to be bored.

Bazaars abound,
State Fairs all around,
Halloween ghosts and goblins appear;
kids are celebrating
this magical time of the year.

HAUNTED

Nestled between towering sycamores,
windows shuttered, locks on the doors.

We bought the house at a bargain price
and moved in boldly, spirits undaunted,
not believing the house was haunted.

Teeming with ghosts, we soon discovered,
shadowy shapes, glimpsed everywhere.

The kitchen was, in earlier days,
the scene of a horrible crime,
we learned this at a later time.

The house juts high on the desolate bank
of a gloomy, murky-water lake,
where fogs and mists hide spectral shapes.

Unexplained noises, outside the house,
and inside, throughout the many rooms.
Footsteps heard, no one is walking.
Murmurings heard, no one is talking.
We couldn't wait to pack and leave.

The house still stands on the eerie shore,
owned by us, and furthermore,
it stands cold, old, and unwanted,
because the house and grounds are truly haunted.

TO AMERICA

Crossing the ocean in 1895,
they were emigrating to America:
a youthful man and wife,
both energetic, full of life.

To Ellis Island, a required stop,
for processing as needed.
Tired now, almost sappy,
bewildered, but very happy.

Transported to the metropolis,
with advice on where to stay,
happened upon a homeless kitty,
would take her on their way.

America.

With their farm plan set
for a destination far inland,
across mighty forests, streams,
to fulfill their long-held dreams.

Wisconsin to be their new home,
joining an Austrian community,
family-members, old-time friends;
immigration will be at its end.

In a few days, they were shown
acres of land to be their own.
With little kitty firmly intact,
and feeling the full impact
of a new farm, it seemed fair.
They all knelt, said a prayer.

116

THANKSGIVING

An enormous moon soars overhead,
bright, full, orange, almost red;
frosty landscapes engulf us tight,
as we drive through the night
at this spectacular time of year,
going home for Thanksgiving.

Rising early the following morning,
we walk out on frozen thatch
to pumpkins lying in their patch.
The apple trees are picked and bare,
Yet, the scent of cider perfumes the air.
The grapes are off the vines,
having been crushed for vintage wines.

Other guests have arrived from the Coast,
invited to dinner by the congenial host,
all looking forward to a festive feast
of young hen turkey or prime-rib roast.
Meanwhile, a colorful table was prepared,
garnishing and trimmings were not spared.

An old-fashioned dinner to be enjoyed,
with apple and pumpkin pies employed;
pans of gravy simmering on the stove,
slowly thickening, brown and murky.
The host's daughter rings a dinner bell,
says, "Come and get it! Roast or turkey?"

After the sumptuous feast is ended,
the dinner table cleaned and bare,
guests are directed to easy-chairs
to discuss current news and local affairs.

While an artistic pair show a sketch they drew,
a scene of the farm's hard-working crew,
and invite the guests to sign it to say,
"Thanks for an outstanding Thanksgiving Day!"

MISSION

Deserted in California,
a strapping young boy
wandered the streets without joy.

Finally, he spied a mission building,
back from the street-side,
where he thought he might hide.
Looking it over, he ventured inside.

"Welcome to the Nineteenth Street Mission,"
said a man, seemingly in charge.
"Are you hungry?" he pleasantly asked.

"Yes," said the boy, "and I'm angry."
"I've been deserted
by traveling companions.
I have no home here."

"Stay here tonight,"
said the man.
"There are chores to do
to make the exchange right."

A year passed, five years,
he stayed on as a regular staff worker,
studied the bible, practiced preaching,
and learned to manage the mission.

After ten years, he was given the position.
He was named the man in charge.
What he had accomplished
was judged very large.

Honored by the community,
he recalled the early years.
Helping those in need
was his daily creed,
especially those feeling deserted.

IMPACT

Memories of a long-ago event.
Memories that seemed,
over the years, to be happily sent
and forever lasting,
as he had married his high-school sweetheart.

He loved her so dearly.
He missed her so clearly.
When the trouble started,
he missed the true impact.
The divorce became an irreversible fact.

EVENING LATE

Once upon an evening late,
fire ashes dying in the grate,
a troubled young man sat
and conjured up his fate.

His recent activities a blur,
largely forgotten, not a lure
that could spark renewed energy
to propel him forward for a cure
for dismal, deadly lethargy.

Sitting quietly, his thoughts un-jelled and unclear,
he spoke out boldly in the empty room,
"I'll go to church and seek a divine, guiding light,
to ease my dreadful mental plight."

Sunday, he heard the message
delivered in the church sermon;
his mind gently sifted the words.
Suddenly, his vision cleared.

As dimness disappeared,
a pressing force descended on him.
He recognized it as a cure for recent troubles,
but from whence it came, he knew not where:
fresh ideas and goals to spare.

BRUSH PRAIRIE

The year was 1885.
The new town of Brush Prairie came alive
with the news that the newly purchased
church bells would soon arrive.

The citizens were anxious
for the bells to be installed.

For the Christmas season,
the tolling of the bells
would serve to foretell
the range of activities occurring
so all the population
could participate in holiday activities.

The church stood on the hill
overlooking the narrow valley.
The bells would sound loud and clear
for all the people to hear.

Installation was completed,
and the new bells were ringing;
the church choir was singing,
"Silent Night, Holy Night"
on Christmas Eve.

This grand performance
capped a profitable year
for the young town of Brush Prairie.

FIRST SNOW

Like petals in a breeze,
snowflakes fluttered,
and quietly fell down
and covered the ground.

Atop the grand hill,
the steepest slope in town,
children gathered around
with sleds to slide down.

Some elders arrived,
built a fire on the crest
for the children's warmth
and a place to rest.

Sliding and gliding,
the sleds were kept busy
with after-school zest
and kids bundled up cozy.

A silent blanket of white
began to crown the trees,
an added gift to sight
to be enjoyed that night.

After darkness settled in,
the fire was extinguished,
sleds gathered by owners,
and all homeward-bound.
Then, not a sound.

WHISTLE

On frigid nights in Winter,
when snow was on the ground,
he would hear the whistle of the train,
as it rushed on through the town.

Thoughts of new, mysterious places
cropped up in his mind.

A wanderlust feeling,
deep down inside,
caused him to utter aside,
"One day, I'll take that ride."

SNOW

From horizon to horizon,
across the wide-spreading valley,
no relief can be found.
Sifting through thick, dark clouds,
snow powders the ground.

Picturesque landscapes
unfold to our sight,
before darkness creeps in
and we prepare for a long night
of snowing and blowing.
We'll wake in the morning,
amazed at Nature's might.

We had earlier moved
to a higher elevation
in the valley to avoid
the low-land air pollution,
but shoveling depths of snow
on a regular basis
discourages this solution.

When Spring finally arrives,
with bright flowers, blue skies,
we'll pack our belongings,
say our goodbyes.

WINTER

The home farm occupies a narrow valley,
circled by ribs of hugging hills,
with lava rocks and ice-age boulders,
set amidst wildflowers and rills.

Autumn season has reached an end;
it's time for a long Winter season again.
Trees have shed their messy foliage;
lawns, gardens, flush with spoilage.

All soon raked clean, bagged, a huge pile
hauled to a dumpsite, nearer a mile.
The growing fields lie bleak, brown and bare;
the harvest equipment stored with care.

Colder, frosty nights now serve warning
that we'll soon awake to a freezing morning;
not long before thick, dark clouds will blot the sky,
winds will bluster, snow will fly.

Snow will deepen throughout the night,
morning landscapes a pleasant delight.
We'll shovel paths early the next day
to bring in supplies needed every day
for the many days of Winter's stay.

This season features the Christmas holidays,
which we celebrate in traditional ways,
always peering ahead, around the bend,
to when plowing starts, and the Winter ends.

CHRISTMAS

Christmas time is once again here:
a special time that welcomes cheer.

We celebrate the birth of Jesus
on that special night in the shelter
of a deserted Bethlehem stable,
as best we can, as best we're able.

The Child was born to the Virgin Mary,
wrapped securely, laid in a manger.
Shepherds guarded the nearby slopes,
because of rumors of the infant's danger.

Three Wise Men traveled from afar,
guided to the baby by a brilliant star.
Could this be the newborn King
rumored for the House of David?

Joseph signed the census scroll,
paid the taxes, while accepting the role
of family protector, until the time
they were safely in Nazareth again.

CHRISTMAS MORN

We heard the bells on Christmas Morn,
they tolled the news that Christ was born.
Church chimes were ringing, too,
as if time would start anew.

Hear the bells, hear the chimes,
important sounds since ancient times.
But hear, also, the mounting din
as we compile wrongs sin by sin.

We hope and pray the newborn Babe,
sleeping in the manger in Mary's care,
is the true and promised Savior lying there.

CHRISTMAS TREE

Oh, Christmas Tree!
Oh, special jewel,
is your symbolism real?

Will the people ever find
peace on Earth
for all mankind?

HITCHHIKING

His name was Niles.
To travel home for Christmas from college
meant hitchhiking 300 miles.
With limited funds, he said, "Yes, I'll try it."

On the highway, rides came fast and easy,
but the weather changed, and it grew colder.
He felt uneasy.

A temperature drop; it could be freezing.
Snow began to fall, and that's not all.
The roads became slick.

A new car pulled up ahead to a stop,
offering a long-mileage hop.

The next he knew, he was speeding down
a slippery highway with a total stranger.
Niles quickly sensed impending danger.

Suddenly a tire blew.
The car swiveled askew,
turning this way and that,
as it left the roadway
and plunged over the side slope of the freeway
into the cold depths of the mountain river.

Niles was screaming.
He awoke in a deep sweat,
sheets were all wet.

He was home in his bed.
"Thank God," he said,
"I took the bus home.
I'm not dead."

PARTY

A party was in full-swing,
Christmas Eve's final fling.
Food, drink and party games;
not a thought for Father James,
saying mass in a nearby church
to celebrate the Infant's birth.

Loud, boisterous people celebrating,
angry voices complaining
about jobs, taxes and daily life
and problems of man and wife,
not a thought or word
about the Virgin Mary
or the Baby lying in a manger.

The party guests don't mention a stable,
not with party snacks
and festive drinks on the table.

NEW YEAR'S

It comes but once a year.
That happens to be January 1.
It is celebrated
with a full schedule of football games.

But Ralph Jones only supports one match,
the oldest bowl game of all:
The Rose Bowl.

Why is that?

It's because the rose is the only flower
he is not allergic to.
Ask his allergist.

Ralph is so grateful, he goes to the game.
But the stadium is full of flowers.
He sneezes the game away.
For some reason,
that makes him happy.

NOSE FOR CRIME

Our young newspaper editor yearned
to write a bestselling mystery yarn.
Plots were simple to find,
but they all fizzled in the end.

He was discouraged,
but one day news broke, just before dawn,
a body had been discovered—
a ravishingly beautiful blonde.

Who deposited her body after dark,
squarely in the middle of the park?

It was quickly learned her name was Gwen.
and nobody could recall when
a body received so much attention.

Our editor had a nose for crime
and detecting of the undercover kind.

His mind led him to the drug scene,
where he learned Gwen had been
active in an import carpet scheme
to launder drug money, where she'd cream
a little off the top to keep for herself.

Our editor had learned why Gwen was dead,
why she'd been bashed on her lovely head,
but failed to find a way to create
a novel plot from this short story.
He continues to wait for writing glory.

OLD SAGE

The editor was respectably and fondly
referred to as the "Old Sage."
Started in the early years,
this friendly rejoinder became a minor rage.

It was bestowed upon him
because of the timely and pertinent advice he gave,
as published in his daily newspaper column.

He received praise and spoken accolades
for hoards of apt phrases and keen advice
he adeptly discoursed, as the years tumbled by.

It was fondly acclaimed that the "Old Sage"
possessed the good sense to match his old age,
but finally the day came
when a mandatory date forced his retirement.

Out of the newspaper, off the editorial page,
the "Old Sage" lived with a festering rage,
and, as what was feared,
he passed on within a year.

From his retirement date,
the newspaper appeared acutely tame,
terribly lame,
never the same,
without the "Old Sage".

FAMILY TREE

Rudy prays that he will never see
an accurate version of his Family Tree.

He traced one branch back three hundred years.
The names that surfaced, for a host of kin,
were all of German origin.

He shudders to trace the ancestry back to earlier days
to learn more of their mean and wicked ways.
I'm sure you'll agree, it would not be fun
to learn that an ancestor was Attila, The Hun.

And none of his family would appreciate
seeing ancestors climbing up and down in the trees,
or in traveling back millions of years,
visualizing original family-members in a slimy mess.

CAMELOT

In Camelot, did Arthur reign,
over hills, moors and treeless plain.
Where wild, pristine rivers ran,
through pastures nurtured by early man,
and tumbled into the sea.
This started Camelot.

Arthur withdrew Excalibur from the stone,
and earned the right to claim the throne.
To rule this green, moody place,
inhabited by people of the Celtic race,
descendants of the ancient tribes.
And Camelot grew.

Peace in the realm, in storied fable,
was maintained by Arthur around a table.
Knights rode in, from near and far,
to settle disputes and avoid war.
Peace in Camelot.

Knighthood was in full flower then,
a noble life for thousands of men.
They raised their cups to wildly cheer
when Arthur wed lithesome Guinevere
to share the Briton's throne.
Powerful Camelot.

Peace and serenity abruptly ended
when Sir Lancelot stated he intended
to steal the affections of the queen
and flee with her from this unsettled scene.
Away from Camelot.

Arthur stepped forth to foil this plot,
banished from the land Sir Lancelot;
placed Guinevere in the Sisters' care,
and retired to his own private lair.
Thus ended Camelot.

BRITONS

King Arthur reigned in Camelot.
The champion Knight of the Realm was Sir Lancelot.
This fighting duo was greatly feared,
rode powerful horses, battle-geared.

Britons they were, in old times named;
as fierce fighters, they were aptly famed.
They fought enemies on every front,
these Britons from magical Camelot.

But internal trouble led to a ban
of Sir Lancelot from the fabled land,
and the retiring of King Arthur
to his private island stand.

Besieged for hundreds of years,
the Britons retreated, to lessen fear,
to lands South and West of Camelot, to where,
if you believe in old wives' tales,
they were in the vicinity of a land called Wales.

CHILD'S TALE

A teacher by trade and underpaid,
he wrote a story for children.
These tales, he was told,
are the easiest to be sold.

Hero. Happy Hound.
Plot unlike any found.
A story to be bought—
that's what he thought.

Mailed the manuscript to a noted publisher.
Manuscript was returned with a short note,
a part of which I quote,
"Not suitable for our type of reader."

He gained control,
in language quite droll,
composed a note
to the publishing house,
a part of which I quote,
"If a story is bad,
just tell me it's bad,
and leave your type
of reader out of it."

COMPUTER

"Are you proficient with the computer?" he asked.
"Yes, no problem," I replied.
"Good. Start by typing your poem onto your template, then run it off for copies," he said.
"No problem," I replied.
"Back in fifteen minutes," he said.
"Excellent," I replied.
In ten minutes, the computer was a total mess.

"How did you manage to do all that?" he asked.
"It wasn't easy," I replied.
"Can we fix it?" I asked.
"No. We'll need to call in our trouble-shooter," he said.
"I'll do it," I replied.
"Goodbye," he said.
"Goodbye," I replied.
Then I crawled into the nearest corner and cried.

IN RHYME

I've written a hundred score,
perhaps a hundred more,
rhyming poems and verses
with but a few mild curses.
But a problem does exist—
first on my personal list:
It's that I'm now speaking in rhyme,
not just once, but half of the time.

And me, with a brand new job,
working for a man named Bob,
as a hardware sales clerk—
not my favorite line of work.
"Yes, ma'am, that's a pliers,
not usually used to cut wires;
you'll prefer this wire-cutter,"
these words I can barely utter.

Oh, when will it all end?
This speaking in rhyme trend?
If it doesn't end very soon,
I'll be pointed out as a loon.

Then, what's even more to be dreaded,
my work will be sent off to be shredded.

PURPLE SHADOWS

Hour after hour of brilliant sunshine passed,
and the first shadows of evening silently crept in,
and in all that time, not a single line
was put to rhyme, by my poet friend.

For the fifth time that day he uttered,
really barely muttered,
"I'm in a slump, not setting goals
or getting any satisfaction from my toils."

Purple shadows quickly invade
the length of the office rooms,
as time for my departure looms.

"Relax," I remark.
"Fresh ideas will arrive with a thump
to propel you over that imagined hump,
out of your slump."

THE GREATEST AMERICAN POEM

Who says I can't write the greatest American poem?
I study this question as I compose here at home.

Competition is keen from famous writers here listed:
Ralph Waldo Emerson, Oliver Wendall Holmes,
Alfred Joyce Kilmer, Wilella Sibert Cather,
John Greenleaf Whittier, Edgar Allen Poe,
and Henry Wadsworth Longfellow.
What about Robert Lee Frost, Carl August Sandburg,
and William Cullen Bryant?

Wait, I have a suggestion—
a quick, final answer to the greatest poem question—
scribble their names, plus many others
on individual slips of paper.
wad them, then drop them
into my quaint wooden shaker.

Shake them thoroughly, then carefully extract
a single name from the shaker.
Don't be surprised as the winning name drawn is
Fredrick Thomas Baker.

REMEMBER ME

Remember me . . .
when Spring flowers
burst into bloom,
bright colors
to chase the gloom.

Remember me . . .
when Summer's sun
is hot and steaming,
fleecy clouds
above are fleeing.

Remember me . . .
when Autumn winds
send leaves dashing
reds, browns, goldens
in Fall's fashion.

Remember me . . .
when Yule time carols
are being sung;
Christmas lights,
bright and gleaming;
gifts exchanged
with faces beaming.

Oh, then,
remember me . . . .